# QUIT SMOKING

If at least once in your life you have thought
that you want to quit smoking but have not
found the courage

**FRANCO TARICONE**

This book will help you to finally be free from the worst prison: smoking. If at least once in your life you have thought about quitting smoking but have not "found the courage", this book is for you. It is a book with 11 chapters about smoking and all its damage to both the human body and the environment. In the book you will also find my story and the experiences of many ex-smokers, accompanied by motivational phrases and tables to fill in to help you on your way. I also recommend a 5-week course accompanied by charts that you can fill in as the weeks go by. At the end of the book you will find notes in which you can enter all your thoughts during the reading of the book and especially during your journey to stop smoking.

Safe and effective, the proposed method is based on my personal experience. This book will accompany you on your path to personal growth and to establish new habits that will help you maintain a healthy and enjoyable life. Risk-free, you will finally be free from cigarette addiction.

acts of their own accord and releases the author and Publisher of any responsibility for the observance of tips, advice, counsel, strategies and techniques that may be offered in this volume.

# Table of Contents

# CHAPTER 1
## Smoking and its damage

Before suggesting ways to quit smoking for good, we need to know what smoking is, why people smoke and the damage smoking does to our bodies and the environment.

When we talk about smoke, we are referring to the process of burning cigarettes (usually tobacco), which is a mixture of gas, steam and various suspended solid particles. Smoke contains around 4,000 substances, although we all know that often only nicotine is mentioned. Of these substances, 700 are considered harmful to health and 69 are considered carcinogenic.

The most recognised toxic/irritant substances released from cigarette combustion include: nicotine, carbon monoxide, acetone, tar, ammonia, hydrogen cyanide and methylamine.

Nicotine is a toxic alkaloid, which can be fatal to humans in very high doses. The effect of the nicotine in cigarettes when you smoke is to increase your blood pressure and raise your heart rate. In addition, if you take nicotine continuously, like cocaine and other drugs, it can cause physical dependence. Therefore, for smokers, nicotine deprivation leads to withdrawal, and its main symptoms are: craving for smoke, anxiety, nausea, headaches, anger, depression and inattention.

Next, we list carbon monoxide. Carbon monoxide is a gas (also known as the gas released by cars). Once inhaled into the human body, it has the ability to bind haemoglobin instead of oxygen.

Therefore, exposure to this gas will result in a decrease in oxygen levels, which are essential for maintaining the survival of various organs in the body. Carbon monoxide is produced when cigarettes are burned. Another important substance released by smoking is tar, which contains about 90 toxic substances produced when cigarettes are burned. After cooling, the tar was yellowish brown. In smokers, the tar 'sticks' to the teeth and fingers that hold the cigarette, turning them yellowish-brown and accumulating in the lungs.

These are the three best known toxic substances in cigarettes and the most harmful substances to the human body and the environment. That said, it is clear that the smoking habit poses a threat to human health. Another very important aspect is that it harms not only smokers but also those around them. Indeed, smoking can be divided into: first-hand smoke (people who smoke directly), passive or second-hand smoke (people who smoke near other people, especially non-smokers), and finally third-hand smoke (still attached Smoking on clothes, hair and objects around us). According to the World Health Organisation (WHO), smoking is a public health problem: more than 7 million people die from smoking and one in two children is a passive smoker.

Smoking affects various areas, involving the respiratory and cardiovascular systems. The consequences of smoking vary from person to person, how cigarettes are consumed and body structure. However, various advertising campaigns have emphasised the health damage of cigarettes, although few people mention how cigarette consumption affects the environment, from processing to product waste. Cigarettes seem harmless because of their size, but the environmental damage of the product is caused by the amount that is discarded every day. Approximately 10 trillion cigarettes are thrown into the street every day. Moreover, as already mentioned, they contain toxic substances that are released into the environment.

In other words, the question arises: why is it so difficult to stop smoking? Why is it so difficult for so many people to kick the habit? As expected, nicotine is an addictive substance that can alter the chemical response of the brain by stimulating pleasurable feelings. What complicates everything is the so-called 'withdrawal syndrome'. When a smoker does not have a cigarette, there will be tension, anxiety and an uncontrollable desire to smoke. Therefore, smoking must be considered a drug in its own right, the difference being that smoking is permitted, just like alcohol.

Another reason why people do not stop smoking is because they claim that cigarettes can reduce stress and anxiety. In the EU, 75% of new cigarette packets are covered with images of vibrations, such as organ disease and warnings about the fatal consequences of smoking. These methods may be impressive, but it may be necessary to shake people up to get them to stop smoking. It is also prohibited to sell thin, flavoured cigarettes, which are particularly attractive to young people. The aim is to make tobacco products less attractive and not to mislead consumers. Tobacco products must look and taste like tobacco, but not have the aroma and attractive packaging required by marketing standards. New electronic cigarettes and herbal smoking products will also adopt new regulations.

An estimated 700,000 people die each year in Europe from smoking-related injuries, which is equivalent to cities like Palermo or Frankfurt. Around 15 billion cigarettes are smoked worldwide every day and 20% of the population regularly consumes tobacco. We already know that smoking can cause damage to the body and the environment, and a large number of studies on smoking have confirmed that smoking can also cause damage to mental health. The aim of this book is to get you to stop smoking, because you will reduce the urge to smoke and smoke as you read each page. Don't try to stop smoking while reading, it is important to read and understand everything.

Thank you for choosing this book! I hope you can find a few minutes to give me your feedback. It means a lot to me. Please leave a 5-star fence on the Amazon page. Best regards!

# CHAPTER 2
## The smoke trap

As we all know, one of the most common ways of quitting smoking for most smokers/ex-smokers is to list the advantages and disadvantages of smoking. Therefore, the person who makes this list quickly realises that the disadvantages are greater and starts to realise that there are no losses when quitting smoking. Usually, after writing down the list of pros and cons, the smoker starts to convince himself/herself that he/she is able to do it. This is an excellent technique by which many people try to stop using tobacco or at least consider using this method every day. In fact, the problem is not quitting smoking, the real problem is the next day, 10 days later or years later.

When you light a cigarette in a vulnerable moment, it causes a strong addiction, so you start lighting it. The desire for another cigarette begins. There you go, you are a smoker again.

Every day there is a lot of information about the effects of tobacco on our bodies, much of which leaves a deep impression on people. Despite this attempt to ask the smoker to stop smoking, you will immediately see him or her light up another cigarette. This happens because fear is usually transmitted to us, making it more difficult. People continue to smoke because of stress. The real question is: why do we want to or have to do it? We have to start forgetting why we want to quit smoking and we have to answer the following questions:

Does it benefit us? Is it necessary to keep spending my life buying something that is bad for me? Do I really enjoy smoking? The fact is that cigarettes have not brought us any benefits. Most smokers think it is necessary to explain why they smoke, but the reality is that they have invented false and misleading stories to convince themselves. If a smoker realises that there is no such thing as a wise and false explanation as to why he or she smokes, then he or she will realise that not only does quitting involve no sacrifice, but there is also plenty of life for non-smokers. More beautiful, better, including more money and better health. All these ideas will help you to understand what life will be like once you have freed yourself from the shackles of tobacco.

All smokers want to quit smoking, even if they don't admit it. Ask them if they want their children to start smoking one day and the answer is always "no". The world of smoking is absurd. The only reason people start smoking is because there are a thousand people who smoke. Imagine a world without smokers: who would take up smoking? No one. On average, a smoker spends about 500,000 euros a day on cigarettes during his or her lifetime. And what is all this money used for? It damages our lungs and poisons our circulatory system. Do you really want to lead a dirty life, full of teeth and smoke?

The serious problem with smoking is that it is in people's minds. When he smokes, the smoker will do his best to stop smoking, if he has the opportunity to go back and not start smoking, he will smoke. But when he went back, he would give him something for the cigarettes. But how does it work? ! Most smokers die without realising that they are addicted to cigarettes, real addicts. Smokers say they do it for fun, but they are fooling themselves. What is so enjoyable about inhaling smoke? Try asking a smoker, when he cannot find a brand of tobacco he likes, he smokes. There is only one bad smoker.

Most people start smoking and become "cool" from children to adults. Many people use "smoking to relax" as an excuse, but they know they are committing suicide and spending money. They simply have no value to admit it. Others have said they did it because their friends did. Do you really want to destroy your lungs and make yourself look cooler in front of friends who may never hear from you again in several decades? Most smokers conclude that they do it out of habit. But this is not a wise explanation; it is still an excuse. Why continue to develop the deadly habit we wish to eliminate from our lives? Once you understand the real reason for smoking, you will stop smoking. If you are honest with yourself, you always do. After a few weeks, the only question is why you didn't stop earlier.

Although millions of people have lost their lives, tobacco is a recognised addictive behaviour worldwide. In order to control the use of tobacco, its sales and promotion must be regulated. Therefore, tobacco cannot be treated as a simple hand cream because it kills and hurts people. The freedom to decide whether to smoke has become an irresistible trap. But from the moment a person starts smoking, that is when they decide to be free and start a life full of smoke. Why does tobacco trap us? Because it is a product specifically designed to create employees, it can be turned into a normal customer. To this end, the goal is to have as many employees as possible in as little time as possible (usually at times when people are most sensitive).

Many marketing campaigns have been created specifically to influence responsible, sensual and mature smoking and even to associate smoking with femininity/masculinity.

The real trap is that our freedom has nothing to do with advertising and marketing, but with toxic substances. The smoker has reached the point where everything depends on tobacco. If you have cigarettes left, you will be anxious because you have to buy more immediately; if the tobacco broker closes, you will be angry because you have to smoke immediately. I mean, is this the life you want? Does your life depend on whether you smoke or not? Spending money? !. Quitting smoking is not necessarily a sacrifice, but people often struggle with addiction. So how do you get rid of this trap? Simple! Quitting smoking is very simple. Start by finding an alternative to smoking, something that makes you feel good instead of ruining your lungs. It has to give us well-being and happiness. Quitting smoking does not mean giving up pleasure, otherwise sooner or later you will end up smoking again in order to feel that "pleasure" we have created in our heads and end the pain. Why? Because smokers associate the moment of smoking with a moment of pause. I smoke to stop thinking, I smoke to distract myself, I smoke to relax. What happens is that, in addition to the addiction, when you stop smoking, there will be no more breaks, so at the moment you need a rest, a moment of stress, sooner or later there is the risk of this relapse. We have to think that quitting smoking is not a loss, but a gain. Throwing away 700 euros is not the same as collecting money, right? . If you want to feel full, you have to take care of yourself. When you talk to a smoker and ask him why he didn't quit smoking, he doesn't want to talk about it, otherwise he will quickly change the subject. This happens because they do not admit that they have a problem and cannot solve the problem, in fact they are unwilling.

Most people use the excuse that they have no willpower and therefore don't stop smoking. But it's not about willpower, it's about admitting to yourself that you have to do something before it's too late. You have to make up for 'lost' time, you have to recover your happiness. It is not true that smoking calms you down and makes you happier, on the contrary, you have a burden inside because you know you are doing something wrong. The way we eat, the way we take care of ourselves, the relationships we establish with other people, that gives us the opportunity to recover the happiness lost with tobacco.

For many people trying home remedies, quitting smoking is very difficult. However, smoking remains the leading cause of death in Europe. So how to break the addiction? Many people are afraid to quit smoking because they think they might gain weight. In fact, nicotine reduces the appetite, but it will affect the resting metabolism, so most smokers (especially women) will gain 3-4 kg. In any case, this weight gain is much more serious than continuing to smoke, and there is a better solution, because once the effects of anxiety and, above all, nicotine addiction disappear, weight is lost.

Quitting smoking doesn't have to mean gaining weight, in fact there are people who start a healthy lifestyle when they quit. Smoking doesn't mean you'll lose weight, so if you started smoking with that in mind, you're wrong. No doctor in the world would recommend a weight loss product that could cause different types of cancer in the body.

The basic principle is: to be able to calm down without smoking and to stop smoking without stress.

The biggest fear of smokers when quitting is the pressure they might cause later on. It is true that moderation can result in anxiety, depression and insomnia, although this obstacle can be overcome with the right measures. At the moment you can quit smoking without going crazy. You may want to know how to simply use the most suitable tool: your mind. You can quit smoking without drugs, all based on psychology. Analyse your thoughts. You have to be distracted and understand your thoughts. When you want to smoke, take all measures to distract yourself. At that moment the anxiety of wanting to smoke intensifies.

People seek smoking to escape from personal problems. Most people think that if they start smoking, they will forget everything at that moment. The truth is that smoking does not reduce stress, it is you who convince yourself that you need something to escape from your problems. But there are many other things you can do on a daily basis without the need to ruin your body: physical activity, cooking, reading, drawing and many others. So why do you resort to smoking to avoid stress? It all starts with the mind. Smoking doesn't actually reduce stress; on the contrary, it worsens it and makes you slowly want more cigarettes. Does that sound like stress reduction to you? Do you feel anxious because you forgot your cigarettes? It seems to be one more problem, so let's try to remove this problem.

# CHAPTER 3
## Tobacco addiction

Smoking has not only become a habit, but also a kind of gambling, a disease that can cause physiological changes in the brain. In addition, it can cause many diseases. There are three types of tobacco addiction: physical, psychological and social.

When we are physically or temporarily dependent, we absorb the effects of nicotine every time we smoke and this effect will soon be felt. It gives us a feeling of happiness, we enjoy it and it soon starts to disappear. This, together with repeated smoking, explains the cause of nicotine addiction. In this way, the nicotinic receptors have to take up a daily dose of nicotine, which can cause a strong addiction to tobacco and nicotine.

In addition, physical dependence on cigarettes is associated with withdrawal syndrome, which is caused by a sharp decrease in nicotine in the body compared to smokers. As a result, symptoms such as anxiety and recent memory loss begin to appear. It should be made clear that these symptoms do not necessarily appear, and many people who quit smoking do not have all the symptoms. We have to remember that every situation is different.

Psychological dependence refers to the association of daily activities with tobacco: waking up in the morning, drinking coffee, talking on the phone; these are all recorded as tobacco-related activities in the brain. It becomes routine. In these situations, cigarettes are the perfect choice because nicotine releases a substance called dopamine. This substance is a neurotransmitter, which is released by the brain every time we do something pleasurable. In this way, nicotine will increase happiness and make people who consume nicotine more relaxed and happy. This makes smokers think that they cannot do without cigarettes.

It should be established that psychological dependence also varies from person to person and, because of its complexity, its duration is much longer than physical dependence.

Tip: To complete this step, we need to change the routine. We need to change everything we do in a day related to smoking behaviour and, most importantly, we need to replace them with other habits. This could include exercise. By participating in a sport you tend to take better care of yourself, which will reduce the urge to smoke. If you really don't want to exercise, there are plenty of other activities that could stop you from smoking: cooking, cleaning, painting, dancing, performing, etc.

Social addiction is related to social pressure and relationships. In many places, people and the environment will smoke.

This is why it is important to consider what measures can be taken in those situations to avoid smoking without being affected, especially when we decide to quit smoking.

There are many questions when you decide to quit smoking. Should I stop or not? But do you remember how you started smoking? Of course, at some point in your life, you are not mature enough to know what you are doing. At that moment, you have decided not to know that you started another life, and it has many faults in the first place.

After smoking for so many years, it becomes more difficult to decide to quit smoking. The first idea is failure, because we need it. In fact, we don't, we don't need it, only habit and dependence.

Usually, we stop smoking when we are pregnant, sick or when someone close to us is ill. Sometimes people are not confident enough to say 'it is time to quit'. You need a lot of motivation. You need to want it very much to be able to do it. Everyone can quit smoking for good. Once you have decided to quit smoking and live a better life, what are you going to do? Well, let's start with the goal, for example, to cut down on one cigarette a day. In this way, if you smoked 20 cigarettes a day, your consumption should be zero within 20 days. One thing you absolutely must understand is that you must forget to give up tobacco and have it back on special occasions such as parties, weddings or celebrations. Don't! . This leads to relapse. When you smoke again, you will start to feel all these sensations and, as a result, you will gradually start smoking 20 cigarettes a day.

eCigarettes are not a way to stop smoking, on the contrary, even if this type of electronic cigarette docs not contain the same amount of toxic substances, you will continue to destroy your lungs with vapour. Let your lungs breathe! They are not used to replace cigarettes because they still contain nicotine and are very addictive. Obviously they seem to be less harmful, but they are still uncertain. In any case, if your goal is to quit smoking, we advise you to avoid smoking. After you have decided to quit, make sure you get rid of any tobacco/lighters/ashtrays that might be nearby. After that, set a date/time to quit and talk to your friends or close relatives, and they will help you.

Note. Before facing this change, you need to understand yourself. If you have tried to go out but failed, consider why you started again, your weaknesses and make this time different. Think of this as a decision you won't regret. If you are here and reading this, this is already an important milestone.

We need to break the connection between cigarettes and tobacco and our daily activities and relationships. Daily activities would include simply getting up every morning. Many people think that getting up is related to smoking one or more cigarettes. We can make sure that there are no identical routines and change the order. This would mean not associating the time of day with smoking different cigarettes. Furthermore, if we exercise and eat correctly, the desire to smoke will decrease. When we take care of our bodies, we do not want to introduce toxic substances, so this is one way to reduce the desire for cigarettes.

You can turn to people close to you who have quit smoking and are now living a healthy life. They will certainly be able to give you lots of advice and help you through the process.

If people close to you do not know that you smoke, you can turn to many web pages that help you in the process and you can do group therapy. Many people prefer to have support and not go it alone.

Starting smoking is not easy, but quitting is even more difficult. Don't start to feel more connected to society, don't damage your body.

This is repeated more than once in the book because it is important that you understand how much you are putting your life and the lives of those around you at risk. If you don't want to quit for yourself, do it for yours. There are many myths surrounding smoking, but only one is certain: it's bad for you!

Smoking is also bad for the skin, so smokers will also look a few years older, with expression lines and wrinkles.

# CHAPTER 4
## Reasons to stop smoking

Quitting smoking is not just about making a decision: "I want to quit" "I know I'm hurting myself". Smoking is part of your life and quitting is a process that requires preparation. If you have been smoking for a long time, you need to spend some time thinking about why you smoked, why you started smoking and why you should stop.

You have to analyse why you smoke. Here is a list of possible causes:

- addiction: you know you have an addiction but you also know that you are stronger than a cigarette.
- reduce negative moods: you think that smoking helps you to overcome your most difficult moments, but it

is you who overcome them, not the cigarette.

- stimulation: you feel that cigarettes help you and stimulate you.
- pleasure/well-being: you smoke to feel good and relax.
- routine: you started smoking but now you don't know why you do it. You just keep doing it because you are used to it.

You have to find ONE REASON to quit. Everyone has a different one. We can start by looking at the effects of quitting smoking on the body:

- 20 minutes after stopping smoking, the heart rate returns to normal.
- One day after quitting smoking, the carbon monoxide is eliminated from our bodies and the lungs eliminate the residues produced by smoking.

- Three days after quitting smoking, you start to breathe better as your bronchi start to relax.
- From three to nine months after quitting smoking, coughing and breathing problems improve as the functioning of the lungs improves.
- Five years after quitting smoking, the risk of dying from lung disease is reduced by at least half.
- Ten years after quitting smoking, the risk of dying from lung cancer is similar to that of non-smokers, as is the risk of getting cancer in the mouth, larynx, oesophagus and kidneys.

Isn't it a good motivation to quit smoking? It is never too late to do so.

If you still haven't found the right motivation to quit smoking, make a list of all the benefits and put it in a place where you can read it often. These benefits may include:

- Quitting for the health of people close to you
- No longer dependent on cigarettes
- Breathe better
- avoid premature ageing of the skin
- Losing yellow in teeth
- Preventing diseases
- Earning money

Everyone has different motivations, find your own.

Now that you have the right motivation comes the hardest part: how do I stop now?!

Surely more than once you have thought that you smoke because it 'relaxes you'/'the damage is done'.

One has to overcome the physical addiction one has. Abstinence from tobacco does not mean suffering, some people don't even experience it, or they just experience harassment.

Decide on a day and time to quit smoking and throw away all cigarettes that may be close to you. Some tips you may need are:

- Drink plenty of water
- Find something that makes you feel good and learn to relax without cigarettes.

People don't usually smoke randomly, but do so at certain times of the day, such as when drinking coffee. So every time we see the coffee we feel like smoking.

To make sure this doesn't happen, you need to make changes in your life and replace those times of the day when you think about smoking with others. Another very important thing to do is to tell your relatives or close friends about your decision, so that they can help you not to start again.

To overcome this addiction you can also write on a chart:

- the hours and minutes you smoke
- the situation you are in, who you are with and what you do
- the reason why you are smoking (routine, social, stress, withdrawal, etc.)

It may help you to stop smoking in the places where you do it most frequently, not to smoke after meals and not to accept/offer cigarettes.

The first day you quit smoking is the hardest. I recommend during the day to distract yourself with other things that make you feel good, remember/read the reasons why you want to quit and keep your hands busy with any object.

If you feel like smoking, wait a few minutes, relax and postpone the cigarette. Once you have put it off, start doing something to distract yourself and keep going. The feeling of wanting to smoke does not accumulate during the day, you gradually forget about it.

If you find yourself in a tense or stressful situation that could lead to a relapse, always find something that makes you feel good or think of something nice. Breathe and count to 10. Concentrate on what you are doing and see how you will succeed.

You must not deceive yourself, cigarettes will not help you through these difficult times, only you are the one who solves problems.

IMPORTANT: Never say 'I'll just smoke another one'. NO! Your last cigarette must have been smoked on the day you decided to quit. Under no circumstances should you smoke a cigarette. Remember that you are now a non-smoker.

Constantly think about the benefits you are getting since you quit smoking and encourage yourself not to do it again.

You have to remember that sooner or later you will find yourself in situations in which you were inclined to smoke before, even after the routine has changed. You have to anticipate these situations to overcome the fact that the urge to smoke may appear.

If after a while you start smoking again, don't be discouraged, losing a battle does not mean losing the war.

# CHAPTER 5
## Key points, motivational phrases and table

You can read this chapter whenever you need to review the key points that can motivate you to quit smoking and also motivational phrases/tables.

Lifestyle motivations:

- You will earn more money
- You won't have to worry about finding a place to smoke
- You won't smell of smoke
- You will breathe better

Health-related reasons:

- The probability of having different diseases is reduced
- You won't have so much coughing
- You will have healthier skin

- No more yellow teeth
- You can practise some sports without fatigue

Motivations concerning family/friends:

- Everyone will be proud of you
- You will become a good example
- You will protect all those close to you

## KEY MOTIVATIONAL POINTS:

1-Better performance in physical activities:

A smoker tends to find it harder to perform any sport than a non-smoker. One of the reasons for quitting smoking is to increase physical performance. Even if you are not used to playing sports, you will notice this in everyday activities (such as climbing stairs).

## 2- Having more time to live:

A smoker lives at least 10 years less than a non-smoker. It is not just that your life may be shortened, it is also the fact that you may spend years in pain. If you stop smoking, over time your lungs will recover and start to function as before. This means that your years of life will increase.

## 3- Improve your physical appearance:

Smoking causes your skin to become drier and age faster. It also causes various dental problems and a tendency to have yellowish teeth. So, if you stop smoking, your aesthetics will also improve.

## 4- Set an example for younger people:

Usually people start smoking when they are young. If you smoke, the message that will get through to younger people is that they can do it too (especially if you have children/grandchildren). If you quit smoking you set an example for the younger generation who are very curious. One of the reasons for quitting is to prevent younger people from falling into addiction like you did.


5-Protecting the environment:

If you smoke, you are contributing to environmental contamination. Both the cigarettes you throw away and the smoke. If you stop smoking, you are doing your home a great favour. We must not forget that the earth is the only home we have.

6-Being more free:

Smoking can be compared to being in a mental prison. If you have a flight, if you are in someone else's car/house, if you are in an area where there are no smoking areas, then you will not feel free and will immediately look for a place to smoke. But what is more beautiful than freedom? If you quit you won't have to worry about what you are doing or where you are.

## MOTIVATION TABLE:

If you don't know whether you are motivated enough, you can try the Mondor test (obviously without being discouraged by a low scorc).

### *Mondor test*

For each of the questions add the indicated points if true or "0" points if false.

1. Points 2
2. Points 1
3. Points 1
4. Points 1
5. Points 2
6. Points 1
7. Points 1
8. Points 1
9. Points 1
10. Points 2
11. Points 2
12. Points 1
13. Points 1
14. Points 1
15. Points 2

Points > 16 very good probability

Points 12-15 good odds
Points 6-11 fair chance
Points < 6 low probability

## MOTIVATIONAL PHRASES:

You think you are smoking, but in reality it is the hand that reaches for the cigarette to tell you the secrets of the lighter.
(Fabrizio Caramagna)

The cigarette is the perfect kind of perfect pleasure. It is exquisite and leaves you unsatisfied. What more could you want?
(Oscar Wilde)

I'm glad I don't have to explain to a being from Mars why every day I set fire to dozens of small pieces of paper and put them in my mouth.
(Mignon McLaughlin)

The cigarette is a tube with a fire at one end and a fool at the other.
(Anonymous)

It has always been my rule not to smoke when asleep, and never to abstain when awake.
(Mark Twain)

God is a Havana smoker. I see his grey clouds. I know he also smokes at night.
(Serge Gainsbourg)

Cigarettes are killers who travel in packs.
(Anonymous)

Thank God, I've stopped smoking again...! God! I feel so fit. With killer instincts, but fit. A different man. Irritable, moody, depressed, rude, nervous, maybe; but the lungs are wonderful.
(AP Herbert)

A good cigar is like a beautiful girl with a great body who also knows the offside rule in front of the television.
(Anonymous).

Eating and sleeping are the only activities that should be able to interrupt a man's enjoyment of his cigar.
(Mark Twain)

Every night, coming back from life,
before this table
I take a cigarette
and I smoke my soul alone.
(Cesare Pavese)

I wonder what people did after love, before they invented the cigarette.
(Vassilis Alexakis)

Smoking kills. But life is no joke.
(Alfredo Accatino)

Quitting smoking is the easiest thing in the world. I know this because I have done it thousands of times.
(Mark Twain)

I quit smoking 3 years, 4 months, 12 days and 27 minutes ago, but I don't think about it at all.
(Anonymous)

Before the discovery of fire, how nervous were smokers?
(Kazzenger)

- Are you smoking?
- No, I'm gonna text Sitting Bull.
(RaF9791)

First God created man, then woman. Then the man pitied him and gave him a cigarette.
(Mark Twain)

I quit smoking. I'm going to live a week longer and it's going to rain in that week.
(Woody Allen)

In crucial trials, the cigarette is a more effective aid than the gospels.
(Emil Cioran)

The best way to stop smoking is to carry wet matches with you.
(Anonymous)

Watching the dance of a cigarette smoke is like watching a girl dance out of her dress.
(DH Mondfleur)

Smoking. One deludes oneself that in this way he is promoting meditation, but the truth is that smoking disperses thoughts.
(Carl Gustav Jung)

As fog, and at best fantastic, which is very different from thinking.
(Cesare Pavese)

I'm trying to quit smoking.
"Have you tried candy?".
"Yes, but they don't light up!"
(Anonymous)

I am trying to quit smoking in stages. For the moment I no longer wear cigarette trousers.
(maxmangione, Twitter)

Could it be that I loved the cigarette so much that I could blame my incapacity on it? Who knows if by giving up smoking I would have become the ideal and strong man I expected? Perhaps it was this doubt that bound me to my habit, because it is a

comfortable way of life to believe oneself
great with a latent greatness.
(Italo Svevo)

# CHAPTER 6
## My story

I started smoking at the age of 13, because of social pressure, I wanted to be the coolest kid. I was very small. One day I went out with my usual group of friends in middle school and one of them threw out his father's stolen cigarettes and lighter. They all started trying and flipping cigarettes to each other. At that moment I didn't want to do it at all, we were all sitting in a circle and I could see the cigarette getting closer and closer to me. I didn't want it to be my turn but, unfortunately, it was my turn. I was shaking with the cigarette in my hand. I was very afraid of what might happen if my parents became aware of this.

As has happened to most of my friends, the first drop sucked. It wasn't a pleasant feeling, in fact I could feel my throat burning and at that moment I couldn't understand how anyone could enjoy smoking. Since then, I have vowed never to touch a cigarette again.

I went on holiday with my parents so I didn't think any more about cigarettes and what I had done, also because I didn't like the feeling at all.

Once back, I saw my group of friends again and got a big surprise: most of them had started smoking stolen cigarettes and exchanging packs as if it was the coolest thing in the world.

At that moment I didn't want to be with them because I didn't feel comfortable but they were also friends that I had known for years and I didn't want to leave. They started telling me that if I started smoking all the girls would come closer and that I would become a man and no longer a child.

So, I decided to smoke only when I was with my group or in front of school so that everyone could see me. Unfortunately, I was not mature enough to make such an important decision and I did not know what I was getting into. I also didn't know the disadvantages and effects of cigarettes on the body. I was used to seeing most adults smoking so I thought that if they did it when they were older and mature then it wasn't so bad and I could do it too.

I started buying the first packs of cigarettes and I was very scared. I didn't know how to hide them from my family because they were very responsible and you couldn't even see these things.

After several outings with my friends, when I got home I realised that I still wanted to smoke a cigarette even though I was no longer with them. I felt the need and convinced myself that it made me feel good.

I started taking the dog out several times a day just to smoke and hide him from my family. After a couple of weeks, I had an addiction to cigarettes.

It was five years ago that I told my relatives that I smoked. I had come of age. Obviously everyone's reaction was to try to help me quit, but I didn't want to give up something that made me feel good. Smoking was now a habit. I smoked when I was sick, when I was well, when I was with my friends, after eating, when I got up in the morning. I had fixed stages in the day when it was compulsory to smoke, otherwise I didn't feel good about myself. It lasted for many years. My relatives had accepted it by then.

When I was 25 years old I was taken to the emergency room by my uncle. I had felt a strong pain in my chest. I was having a heart attack. The doctors told me that smoking was the cause and that if I didn't stop smoking my condition would get worse and worse and I might die.

Fortunately, I am here to tell you my story. From that moment on, many times I decided to stop smoking because I didn't want something like that to happen to me again. I wanted to be healthy. Unfortunately, after several attempts I always ended up smoking.

Smoking was my escape for me, whenever I smoked I took it as a break from stress.

Between so many things like rent, work, love life and so on, I was always stressed and always ended up looking for my only medicine: smoking.

When I was 30 I got engaged for the first time to a girl who smoked. None of my ex-girlfriends smoked.

We had been very well for several years until she started to feel sick and have strange symptoms. When I took her to the hospital we received the worst news that would change our lives forever: she had been diagnosed with lung cancer.

I felt like the world was collapsing on me, I didn't want to lose the love of my life because of smoking.

From that moment on I was so close to her and I couldn't part with her, I didn't know when the last day would be.

The doctors told her that if she continued to smoke the situation would get worse, so she decided to quit because she couldn't take it any more and she was very sick because of the different treatments and chemicals. So I decided to stop because I didn't want to hurt her.

So, we got rid of any cigarette or tobacco near us and started our life again.
At that moment I started to change. I no longer saw smoking as a way out but as the enemy. I promised myself never to smoke again in my life.

Three years had passed and my fiancée was still fighting with cancer. Months later, I took her to the hospital and that time we received the best news of all: she had managed to recover from this cancer and was healthy at last after years.

We started to travel and feel good without smoking.

At the age of 35 my uncle died. I was so close to him. I didn't understand why it was happening to me.

In that moment of so much pain and suffering I was looking for something that would make me escape from that world even if only for a few minutes. Among many choices, I went to buy cigarettes. I made the wrong decision of my life. I promised myself that it would only be that one packet and no more than two cigarettes a day, just to eliminate those moments of suffering.

Once I finished that packet, I ran to buy another one. I convinced myself that I needed cigarettes because they made me feel more peaceful and relaxed, but in reality I was just addicted to them.

When my girlfriend saw me smoking after I had managed to quit with her, she decided to leave me. I understood her. After years of suffering she did not want to go back to the same point. It was a dark period. I couldn't see the way out. I was alone.

These were years of suffering and loneliness where my only companion was smoking.

Four years later I visited a friend of mine whom I hadn't seen for a long time and who was also a mutual friend of my ex-girlfriend. His name came up in conversation and I was told that he had started smoking again.

I left my friend's house and went to look for her. I didn't understand why, after years of suffering, she had started to do something again that would lead to her death. But then again, I was incoherent. The thought that I might lose her or that something might happen to her again because of smoking was unacceptable and I didn't want that.

We talked and mostly argued a lot, but the love was still there and could not be avoided. So, we took the decision to start again, to help each other and to start the journey together. After a few months, we moved in together, eliminating any tobacco/cigarettes that might be near us. I have to admit that at the beginning it was difficult for both of us. But if there was one good thing, it was that we were there for each other.

I strongly recommend that if you want to quit smoking you tell someone close to you. This will make it easier to vent and get help when you need it.

You also have to set goals. Ours was to have a healthy life. We started changing our routines and doing things we had never thought of before to avoid thinking about smoking.

Whenever we thought about wanting a cigarette we tried to postpone it and do something in the meantime. We love to paint and distract ourselves.

I have to admit that in the beginning it was very difficult and there were many relapses on both sides. It's not an easy path. The important thing, however, is that you want to stop and give up hurting yourself.

It helped us to think about what could happen to us if we continued to smoke and especially to think about all the steps we had taken together. I wrote several lists of the pros and cons of smoking and the list of cons was much longer. I didn't want to spend more money, I didn't want to have that addiction anymore.

I noticed with my partner that every path is different. His was different from mine. Yet we both succeeded.

Don't be afraid. You will succeed. Some faster and some slower, but if you want to, you can do it.
Today, it has been five years without having touched a single cigarette.

# CHAPTER 7
## <u>Myths debunked and behaviours to be acquired</u>

III 'Smoking tobacco is not that bad'
In most industrialised countries, tobacco is the leading cause of death. Around 6 million people worldwide die from smoking.

"If I stop smoking I will not be happy anymore".

For smokers, the act of smoking is generally related to happiness. Therefore, when you stop smoking, you may feel that you are missing something. However, as time goes by, this feeling gradually disappears.

"I don't notice that it hurts that much."

Even if the effects of smoking on your body are not immediately noticed, your body is becoming increasingly damaged.

"I'm stressed: the only thing that can help me is smoking.

Normally, a smoker feels a pleasant sensation when smoking, perhaps because the withdrawal effect is weakened, but in fact smoking increases the tension in your body.

"Tobacco is not a drug
Tobacco is a substance that can cause physical and psychological dependence and can cause withdrawal syndrome when not in use, so it is considered a drug.

"It's too late to stop smoking.
This is absolutely not correct. It is never too late to quit. As mentioned above, even

if you have been smoking for many years, if you quit smoking you will immediately notice many changes in your health.

"Only people who have a lot of willpower or who have suffered some kind of illness are able to quit.

Anyone can quit, but we have to remember that what is important is not willpower, but making decisions and having a very clear goal.

Now, having dispelled these myths, let's look at what you need to do while quitting smoking in more detail.

THE FIRST WEEK
During your first week your goal is to know your usual cigarette consumption. The best form is to record your cigarette consumption. You should write down

every cigarette consumed during the day so that at the end of the day you can see how much you consume per day. A tip is to write down the hours you smoke and how much time has passed from one cigarette to another. If you have not smoked in an interval of time, you should write down 0 cigarettes.

Once the week is over, calculate your diary consumption of cigarettes. This will help you visualise how your consumption will start to decrease over the next few weeks, or rather, you will be able to see your progress.

Below is a table to fill in to help you during this week:

## AVERAGE NUMBER OF CIGARETTES SMOKED DURING THE FIRST WEEK:

.................

## SECOND WEEK

This week you have the objective of writing down the reasons why you want to stop smoking and continue with the table this time trying to reduce your consumption of cigarettes per day.

The goal is to reduce your cigarette consumption considerably, so that if last week your average was 20 cigarettes a day, this week you must set yourself a lower average and create your own table. If you usually smoke 15 cigarettes a day, but on that day you smoked 20 cigarettes, you must ensure that on another day you smoke 5 fewer cigarettes to reduce your average.

To make sure you don't smoke more than you should, you can make a deal with someone to pay them if you smoke a few more cigarettes. Trust me, your desire to go over the limit will be greatly reduced. Also, here are some other tips:

- Do not accept if offered cigarettes! the cigarettes you smoke must have been taken by you and not offered.
- When you smoke you can also try smoking only half a cigarette, it doesn't sound like much but it is a great change.
- Remove tobacco from visible areas
- Try smoking with the other hand
- Choose places where you cannot smoke
- Each week you can write down the money you are earning by smoking fewer cigarettes. Later you can use that money to reward yourself.

Here are some tables to fill in that will help you during this week:

## REASONS WHY YOU WANT TO STOP SMOKING:

1- _____

2- _____

3-_____

4-_____

5- _____

6- _____

7- _____

8- _____

9- _____

10- _____

## AVERAGE NUMBER OF CIGARETTES SMOKED DURING THE SECOND WEEK: ..............

## THIRD WEEK

In this week your goals are to continue to reduce the number of cigarettes you smoke per day and to understand why you quit smoking.

Next to each cigarette you smoke, write the reason why (withdrawal, habit, stress, boredom, etc.).

In addition to reducing cigarettes, impose rules that will make it more difficult to increase consumption - during the week you will not be allowed to smoke:

- just got up
- after meals
- in the company of non-smokers (especially children)
- when having coffee or other drinks

As we said in the previous chapter, tobacco is smoked for a different reason each time, depending on the situation you are in. The idea is to eliminate cigarette consumption completely and replace it with something else. Here is a list of what you can do every time you think about smoking:

- Drinking water
- chewing gum
- read
- listening to music
- watching TV
- sleep
- cooking
- manual work
- physical activity

Below is a table to fill in to help you during this week:

AVERAGE NUMBER OF CIGARETTES SMOKED DURING THE THIRD WEEK: ...............

## FOURTH WEEK

This week is the most important one. Here your goal is to quit smoking completely. You have to prepare for the big day.

Choose the day and time you want to quit and start preparing:

- Eliminates everything that triggers the desire to smoke
- Plan what you want to do during the day (if you want to do it during the next few days) to distract yourself from the urge to smoke.

Don't get up that day thinking that you are going to stop smoking for good, as drastic and permanent changes put us under great strain. Rather, every morning when you get up think "I'm not smoking today". This will help you at the end of the day to see if you have achieved your goal.

During the first few days without smoking you feel a strong desire to smoke. This will cause increased anxiety and nervousness during this time (not everyone does this). At times when you are very nervous and have a strong desire to smoke you can:

- carry out some of the activities on your list
- going for a walk with relatives/friends/children/dogs
- think about the reasons for quitting
- focus your attention on something else

During these days do not forget to reward yourself for your achievements.

Below is a table to fill in to help you during this week:

LIST OF THINGS TO DO/THINGS THAT DISTRACT ME:

1- _____ _____

2- _____

3- _____

4- _____

5- _____

6- _____

7- _____

8- _____

9- _____

10- _____

## FIFTH WEEK

Now you become an ex-smoker.

With time you will get used to enjoying things without the need to smoke. You will probably feel sadder or different but these are normal feelings during the first few days. Think how far you have come!

Help yourself find new sources of satisfaction, or rather, increase activities that make you feel good about yourself.

But, what happens if I start smoking again?

Certainly one of the things that will worry you most this week is the fear of returning to smoking. First of all you only need to worry about not smoking on a day-to-day basis. Then you have two different concepts: fall and relapse.

The moment of the fall is when an ex-smoker smokes a cigarette again after a long time without having done so. Relapse is when an ex-smoker resumes the habit of constant smoking.

If you produce the first one, you have to recognise that that cigarette was a mistake. Secondly, you have to resume your goals as an ex-smoker, namely not to smoke.
If there is a relapse, you need to know that there are reasons why this happens:

- stressful situations

- parties, weddings and other social events
- boredom
- anxiety and/or nervous situation
- What you can do is try to imagine yourself in these situations and what you could do to solve it and not fall into temptation.

A table to be filled in (in case of a relapse) follows:

REASONS WHY I DID IT AGAIN:

1- _____

2- _____

3- _____

4- _____

5- _____

6- _____

7- _____

8- _____

9- _____

10- _____

How are you finding the book? If you want to help more people buy it and quit smoking, leave your opinion and 5 stars on the Amazon page.

# CHAPTER 8
## Different experiences

Matthew, 32 years old
"I quit several times and went a few years without smoking. But now I'm smoking again. One piece of advice I give you is to really want to quit smoking. If you really want to quit you will succeed, even if you go through bad times. If you don't want to quit, you can't fool yourself, you won't. Quitting smoking is mental, not physical: the secret is the MIND."

Jade, 26
"Quitting smoking is a matter of wanting to, whether with or without help from anyone. I have quit smoking several times in periods, I have gone up to two years without touching a cigarette. Sooner or later, however, I would always start again. What always happens to me is that when

I'm with friends at a party, a wedding, a park, they offer me a cigarette and in order not to say no, you end up accepting it and you think: "One cigarette and that's it". You think that with that cigarette you're not going to start again, but instead....

My advice is not to accept cigarettes, even if your friends insist. Trust me, you are making the best choice. With time you will realise that smoking will do you no good and you were only harming yourself. I haven't smoked for three years and have no intention of taking it up again. I feel better about myself, healthy and carefree. The best part was earning the money".

Luca, 55
"I have been an ex-smoker for 10 years now. Honestly, I have never felt so addicted to tobacco that I couldn't quit, so

it was easy for me. I believe that addiction many times turns into obsession and illness. In many cases you have to get help and the first thing is to accept it. I didn't need any help at all and I decided to quit overnight. Since that day, I have never touched another cigarette.

Mario, 38
I started smoking when I was 16. I stopped smoking when my wife got pregnant and I was 27, but soon after that I started smoking again.

Last year I set out to quit smoking but it was very difficult for me. I tried to reduce the number of cigarettes pcr day but never quit completely.

One day I discovered a packet of cigarettes in my son's rucksack. I knew very well the harm of smoking and the addiction it can cause, so to see my son start like I did was painful. After that day I stopped smoking completely. I didn't want to be a bad influence on my son and I felt guilty that he started smoking because he saw me do it. Today I am 38 years and 10 months without smoking.

Lucia, 23

"I am young, but I started smoking even younger, at the age of 14. At the age of 20, my brother fell ill from smoking and from that moment on I noticed that smoking was not my friend but my enemy. I never realised how dangerous a cigarette was. I always smoked without being aware of the damage I was doing to myself. I only opened my eyes when my brother was ill. Now I haven't smoked for three years and I'm expecting a baby.

Miriam, 47

"I only tried a cigarette when I was 17 but I have never smoked. However, I am surrounded by smokers/ex-smokers in my family and I wanted to tell you a bit about what I know and their experiences. Both mum and dad used to smoke more than two packets of cigarettes a day, while my brother still smokes about one and a half packets of cigarettes a day.

Most people get help with medication or something like that, but I actually think the problem with smoking is mental. The physical effects of addiction go away with time, the problem is mental addiction. You start to think that you can't do anything without smoking a cigarette and that you can't do without it.

People who really want to stop smoking do it. Mum and Dad did it because they were noticing changes in their health and physique and wanted to take it seriously.

My brother tried several times but only managed to go four months without smoking. You need to be completely convinced of the decision you want to make and be aware that that decision will change your life for the better. I recommend quitting smoking suddenly and never smoking again, that's what worked for mine. The first few days my parents struggled and it was hard physically, but after that it becomes more of a mental thing.

I also have the feeling that more anxious people need tobacco more and cling to it to escape from anxiety. Calmer people have less difficulty because they don't have as much addiction. I noticed this when I watched my parents quit smoking. For my father it was more difficult to quit, he is too anxious, whereas my mother is calmer and it was easier. I don't know if it's right or wrong but that's what I've noticed. It doesn't necessarily mean that if you are anxious you can't quit, on the contrary, everyone has completely different experiences when it comes to quitting smoking.

Giusy, 21
"This is what I did to stop smoking.
First I decided on a day and also the time when I wanted to quit smoking. It was very difficult for me to quit smoking thinking that it would be forever. Therefore, when I quit I told myself that I would quit for 3 years. Now I haven't smoked for 5 years. I was small when I started.

Secondly, I rewarded myself: with the money I earned during one year I bought myself a phone. I started to hate tobacco and realised how lousy it was and how much I was losing from it.

One piece of advice I can give you is to choose the day you want to quit smoking especially during the holidays. During those times you won't be stressed and it will be easier for you to quit. The main thing is to really want to quit. If you don't want to do it, honestly, even with medication you won't be able to do it".

Marika, 30
"I am not a smoker but I know a gentleman who is and I sincerely wanted to make an appeal to smokers. This gentleman smokes in front of his children who are both very healthy. My son has cancer and he is lucky enough to have two healthy children and he makes sure that those children breathe in the smoke that he lets out. I hope that many of you with this

message realise that life is two days and that we have to make the most of it by not harming our bodies and the people around us. So I hope that everyone who reads my message will realise that health is the most important thing. Stop hurting yourself!"

Martina, 36
"I haven't smoked for four years.
Initially, when I heard about methods to quit smoking, the first thing I thought was that it wouldn't work for any reason. Then I tried the method of stopping smoking gradually and it worked. I couldn't believe it, I had finally managed to quit smoking, something that was only hurting myself. I'm very proud of myself and if I can do it, I know you can too. STRENGTH!"

## Gian, 18

"I started smoking when I was 12. I know, very young. Luckily I realised now that I am still young how bad smoking is and how much damage I am doing to my body. My case is very special. My father had an addiction to hard drugs like cocaine, he forced me to be like him. He started forcing me to smoke when I was 12 years old. Luckily I managed to escape, otherwise I wouldn't know where I would be now. I grew up in a world where syringes and drugs were normal. So tobacco meant absolutely nothing to me. I had to go through various therapies for the trauma it caused but I never started smoking again. I am now disgusted by smoking. Every time I think of smoking I think of my father, what he made me do and the conditions he was in. I think once you hate tobacco you won't touch it and you'll never want to see it again.

Matthias, 56

"I smoked about two packets of cigarettes a day. One day my chest hurt a lot and I went to the hospital: I was having a heart attack. From that moment on, I wanted nothing more to do with cigarettes. I went many years without smoking, but slowly I started to get addicted again, until I was smoking two or more packs again. When I got to that point I decided to quit again, this time in a radical way. Today I have not smoked for 20 years.

Michelle, 24

"I became a vegetarian and started to do a lot of physical activity. Over time I noticed many changes in my body, but all I needed to do was stop smoking. I felt the need to stop smoking because I didn't feel 100 per cent healthy. I was getting very tired and I also discovered I had asthma a few years ago. One day out of the blue I decided to quit for good and that was it.

Laura, 60

"I tried several times to quit smoking but for some reason I always started again. The fourth time I quit smoking was the decisive time for one reason: I had found out that my friend's son had died of lung cancer."

Eva, 40

"I started smoking to please my friends when I was 13. I felt very cool and fashionable. The truth is that I was just a little girl afraid of not being accepted by society. I didn't know the mistake I was making and only realised it a few years ago. The more years went by, the more I smoked all kinds of cigarettes. One day I smoked 40 cigarettes. I was really losing control.

My family realised what was happening to me and they took me to therapy. In my opinion it was the best choice they could have made. I met a lot of ex-smokers who helped me along the way and today I have been smoke-free for five years. I think the key to quitting is to see cigarettes as an enemy."

Marta, 34
"I smoked for 10 years. I smoked too much and my family kept telling me that I should stop, I was overdoing it. One day I realised after watching a documentary how important it is to take care of yourself. So, I ran to the kitchen where I had all my cigarettes and stuff and I just threw them away. It may seem like a random decision, but I haven't smoked since then.

## Michael, 23

"I haven't smoked for four weeks today. I saw some tickets to New York a few weeks ago and I thought the price of the tickets was absurd. Then my girlfriend pointed out to me that it was a price more or less close to what I used to spend in 3-4 months on tobacco. Since then I don't smoke anymore and I'm earning that money to go to New York with my girlfriend."

## Fabio, 39

"I never wanted to stop smoking, in fact I always enjoyed it and I never noticed any changes on my body due to smoking. I went to the hospital to get tested as I do every year on a regular basis and they told me they needed to do more in-depth tests. From that moment on I got scared and decided to quit for the sake of my health and those around me. Take this as an encouragement to do it before it's too late."

Luciano, 21

"I started smoking a few years ago because I was suffering from panic attacks and anxiety. A friend of mine had told me that cigarettes helped him to feel more peaceful and calm so I decided to give it a try myself, I was really sick and had nothing to lose. As the days went by my attacks got much worse and I went to the doctor. The doctor told me that smoking had increased the risk of having these attacks and that I absolutely had to stop. I decided to give up cigarettes. I had never been addicted to them, I simply wanted to feel more relaxed. Fortunately, I stopped smoking immediately."

# CHAPTER 9
## <u>The main reasons for failure</u>

1.  I rely on willpower.

    Many people believe that change and willpower must be combined. Smoking is an addiction, and changing this habit requires not only willpower but a series of steps to be followed.

2. You chase methods that do not work for you.

    There are many methods to quit smoking, you just need to find the one that suits you best. Not all of them are effective or 100% guaranteed. It is not recommended to follow methods that promise to stop smoking in a day or in a short time. Quitting takes time and, above all, a desire on your part.

## 3. Lack of reasons to stop smoking.

All changes in life require effort, and not everyone is willing to make them. However, if you ask a smoker if they want to quit, the most likely answer is yes.

## 4. You feel dejected by the treatments already carried out.

As has been said before, all equal beings are different. What doesn't work for you might work for someone else. You simply have to look until you find something that is right for you. It is normal to think about giving up. The important thing is to always have the will to try again and not to think that no one will work for you. If you are pessimistic you are already assuming that the treatment will not work and that you will fail. If this happens to you, it is advisable to see a psychologist for help and improvement.

## 5. Side effects of quitting smoking

When nicotine is removed from our bodies, they become active and adapt to the situation. Usually we feel more tired and anxious. You should not be afraid of these effects: they are a sign that your body is changing and adapting to living without smoking again. Beyond that, the side effects go away after a few weeks.

## 6. You are afraid of gaining weight.

Some people increase their appetite when they stop smoking and especially try to replace smoking with food. But increased appetite can be caused by changes in the body, such as an improved sense of smell. This does not mean that all people have to deal with weight gain when they stop smoking. If this happens to you, it is advisable to always have plenty of fruit and water nearby. Remember that smoking is more harmful to your health than gaining weight, so quitting smoking should be your priority.

## 7. You don't know how to control your anxiety

If you are very anxious and don't know how to control your anxiety if it is not smoking then you probably can't quit because of it. Smoking has a calming effect for a short time and you probably smoke to feel calmer and not have anxiety. Try to find something to replace smoking. Something that makes you feel good, calms you down and that you can do in times of anxiety (drawing, cooking, etc...).

## 8. Confusing a fall with a relapse

Many people confuse a fall with a relapse and therefore give up and start again. As mentioned in the previous chapters many of the attempts to quit smoking fall apart when you have smoked again. You become despondent and think that you have failed in your attempt to quit smoking. These episodes of falling down are normal. It means picking up the cigarette again in times of difficulty or stress. What you need to do is to set your goal again the next day. A relapse, on the other hand, is to start smoking again and becoming addicted to the cigarette. If you have relapsed, don't get discouraged, find your own method and start again.

## 9. You donot pay attention to small successes

You probably create very difficult goals for yourself and don't pay attention to the small progress you make. It is much easier to create daily goals and achieve them day by day. As already mentioned, you can fill in the tables in the previous chapters to help you regulate your tobacco consumption.

**10.** You donot feel the help of the people around you

In order to quit smoking, it is important to have the help of the closest people around you. Quitting smoking is certainly easier if the people we love help us and support us in our decision. Many times because of unsuccessful attempts, close people make jokes about your failures or keep telling you that you won't make it or you won't last long. It is up to you to decide whether to beat yourself up over this or to make it an extra motivation. Or there may be smoking people around you who make it more difficult. Look for positive people to help and support you, especially people in the same situation as you. If it is not easy for you to find these people, you can use group therapy for people who want to quit smoking. You can find them both in person and online.

## 11. You donot give weight to your health benefits

Many times we don't realise the benefits of quitting smoking and therefore don't give it much thought. Quitting smoking, even if you are already of an advanced age or have been smoking for many years, still has positive effects on your body as soon as you quit and reduces the chances of having diseases that can be fatal to your body.

## 12. You donot realize changings in your surroundings

Many times quitting smoking means making changes in your daily routine to avoid falling back into the temptation to smoke. Among these, smoking at coffee time is very common. In this case, you can try to change the time you drink coffee, or eliminate it and replace it with another drink. Also, many times people find themselves in times and circumstances when they feel compelled to smoke. Try to eliminate those circumstances in your daily life. Avoid smoking rooms and never accept cigarettes offered to you.

# CHAPTER 10
## Summary

Chapter 10 will be a summary of how to stop smoking. To be re-read every time you start again or feel like starting again.

All you have to do is decide that you will not smoke any more.

You're probably wondering what's the point of reading the whole book if there's a summary here. Yes, but before you can stop smoking, you have to understand what you are getting into. You can only understand this by reading the whole book with its explanations. Once you have read it, you can go over the most important points in this summary.

## POINT 1
## UNDERSTAND THAT YOU CAN DO IT.

The only person who can decide whether or not to continue smoking the next cigarette is you. Get it into your head that you can do it, as many have done.

## POINT 2
## DECIDE WHEN TO STOP.

From the moment you decide to quit you have to know that there is no turning back. If it is difficult for you to think that you will never smoke again, try setting yourself a time limit (no smoking for 5 years...etc) and you will find it easier.

## POINT 3
## ALWAYS HAVE A POSITIVE ATTITUDE.

Don't think that you will suffer or that you will feel bad because of the addiction, instead think "how nice! From today I am a non-smoker!". This will make it easier for you to continue on your path.

POINT 4
AWARDED.
Every time you make a goal during your route (especially during the weekly route) reward yourself even with a small detail. With this method you will be more and more eager to achieve the reward and you will continue to make goals.

POINT 5
THINK OF THE BENEFITS.
Never think that you are giving up something, otherwise you will see it as something negative. Instead, think about the immense benefits of quitting smoking.

POINT 6
LOOK AT SMOKING AS A DRUG ADDICTION

If you conceive of smoking as an addiction, then you won't want a single cigarette. You have to get out of that circle. If you touch another cigarette you risk going back to the way you were before.

## POINT 7
## THINK YOU WERE SICK WHEN YOU SMOKED

Theoretically, when you smoke you are 'sick' because you are bringing toxic substances into your body. Remember that smoking not only harms you but also makes you worse over time. Your time to get well has come.

## POINT 8
## NOT GIVING IN DURING THE ABSTINENCE PERIOD

It is very important that during the maximum 3 weeks of abstinence you do not give in for any reason. That way you will give way to mental dependence, and then it is up to you to decide whether to quit or not. Of course this step will be easier for you if you have the right mental attitude.

## POINT 9
## DON'T FEEL DOWNHEARTED

You have absolutely no need to fear that you are not strong enough to cope. We have already said that smoking is a trap. Everyone can fall into it, but it is up to you not to keep falling back into it after discovering it.

Thank you for choosing me! If you enjoyed reading it and would like to leave your own review you can go to the amazon page and leave a 5 star review.

# CHAPTER 11
## <u>Notes</u>

_____

_____

_____

_____

_____

_____

_____

_____

_____

_____

_____

_____

_____

_____

_____

_____

_____

_____

_____

_____

_____

_____

_____

_____

_____

_____

_____

_____

_____

_____

_____

_____

_____

_____

_____

_____

_____

_____

_____

_____

_____

_____

_____

_____

_____

_____

_____

_____

_____

_____

_____

_____

_____

_____

_____

_____

_____

_____

_____

_____

_____

_____

_____

_____

_____

_____

_____

_____

_____

_____

_____

_____

_____

_____

_____

_____

_____

_____

_____

_____

_____

_____

_____

_____

_____

_____

_____

_____

_____

_____

_____

_____

_____

_____

_____

_____

_____

_____

_____

_____

_____

_____

_____

_____

_____

_____

_____

_____

_____

_____

_____

_____

_____

_____

_____

_____

_____

_____

_____

_____

_____

_____

_____

_____

_____

_____

_____

_____

_____

_____

_____

_____

_____

_____

_____

_____

_____

_____

_____

_____

_____

_____

_____

_____

_____

_____

_____

_____

_____

_____

_____

_____

_____

_____

_____

_____

_____

_____

_____

_____

_____

_____

_____

_____

_____

_____

_____

_____

_____

_____

_____

_____

_____

_____

_____

_____

_____

_____

_____

_____

_____

_____

_____

_____

_____

_____

_____

_____

_____

_____

_____

_____

_____

_____

_____

_____

_____

_____

_____

_____

_____

_____

_____

_____

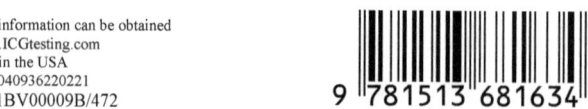